Second Nature

John Schertzer

SPUYTEN DUYVIL

New York   Paris

Acknowledgements

Versions of the poems collected in this manuscript have appeared in *Big Other, Cortland Review, American Letters and Commentary, The Germ, 1913 Journal vol 6, Danse Macabre, Inverted Syntax, LIT, 6,500, Terra Incognita* and elsewhere.

ISBN 978-1-956005-94-3

Library of Congress Cataloging-in-Publication Data

Names: Schertzer, John, author.
Title: Second nature / John Schertzer.
Description: New York : Spuyten Duyvil, [2022]
Identifiers: LCCN 2023000180 | ISBN 9781956005943 (paperback)
Subjects: LCGFT: Poetry.
Classification: LCC PS3619.C3497 S43 2022 | DDC 811/.6--dc23/eng/20230106
LC record available at https://lccn.loc.gov/2023000180

To Kathleen

CONTENTS

SECOND NATURE

FRONT

You were born with a rumor
(to smell and taste and say)

And everything issuing from that point
Became a wedding vow to an orchestra seat

The sound that empties your eyes
When one day you would undo

The strong magnetism that compels you

And watch for a new opera
With new impediments
Couples will still be making love on the hill
The smell of dandelions and pungent herbs

Learning to expand and wait
Overwriting what currently endures

Until like a story teller drifting in a healed world asks
What shall you do and what shan't you

The Crawl

If not for this landing, the crime would be adorable
pursing lips at possible motives—
a stolen pony from a carousel

driven into the ground in search of earth.
But why this basket, and why this measuring cup
when you can see I'm already in tears

over the way you danced over
to me to refill my coffee?
I'm no elemental as you are,

but a rudimentary dawn
to dark played out in biology, as you'd find
on any channel between eight and ten.

But don't lose faith on my account,
since I might trick you,
been tricking myself for years,

don't quite know what to make of me,
and you—most complex mathematical formula,
with a mutable and sticky itinerary, handed down

through wards with webbed feet,
when all the gods were quartz-fisted devils,
whose game of mash and crunch

went on as casually as golf, jokes and cocktails
hatched from thermos bottles
under dark skies, as rain washed away our guts.

But this toy, this wooden animal
sure looks silly, stiff but over-excited, hooves
jammed into the dirt, racing off

to some deadline beneath the surface.
Perhaps this looks too much like therapy,
but let's adjust the lens,

turn it round on its axis, so we
no longer diagram a plummeting throng
of rebel angels or apples, but a chase

where the invisible rider escapes
his doom, flees an army of cartoon villains
into a secret opening of a cave in a cliff side,

where he'll bargain for his life
with the king of the underworld.
But no—this is crooked, it's a delirium.

There are no heroes, no cloaks
of invisibility or disappearing doors—
though not all the forces are visual,

not like you: lips painted, pouting,
or putting on your monkey grin,
pinning me to the floor like you're saddling up

to do damage to the one thing
you've been falling through all your life,
and manage momentarily to forget.

SHADOW WARMER

She was flying out of her raincoat
with shivers running down her face in braids
hands clawing at the phone receiver
on a message mission weeks late
already planetary in its denial of the present
conflagration, the dulled polish of shoes, lots of pots
and plates to wash filling up the sink
to an explosive level. She was never very good
at keeping the odor of things
down to a dull roar. All of her characteristics
blew out of her, like she flew out of her protective layers
leaving the wet garment of inertia
in a puddle on the floor, a history abandoned
by the point at which it meets the future
and vanishes into a carbuncle of presumption.
And so a young man with dead bird parts
attached to the grille of his Duster
watched her slingshot herself out to the mail
one afternoon, as she waited for the rest
of her week to be delivered
in a small box. The blur was almost scientific
and charged his sex glands
with a new form of money, one tasting
like a cheap mai tai, coating his lungs
with a bright yellow light he recognized
from movies about space aliens and possession.

Fuse of Evening
for KeK

We have the dark now. In a letter to her mother
Sounding like a narrow shadow, she said "Welcome

Cloudless night, for instance," and waved her hand
Over a column of incense smoke. The letter rose

Over the coil and spun mechanically as a way
Of explaining. The reflex sat stiffly back in her

Chair. Additional margins were sewn to her collar
And sleeves. She stood up, or was heaved up

To her feet, into the forest fire of her hair. I learned
To balance on a branch and watch her devour and

Regenerate herself, her dancing a meringue with
The soft black fuzz of the evening, humidity and lack

Of moonlight giving off a burnt flavor, as if a fuse
Had exterminated itself, despairing our distance.

Wheels turned and levers flew. She remained inside me
Extended out past my reach, out among the faces

Turned away or masked by the buttress of shadows.
I was willing to talk about almost anything, but she

Was a breeze out of the lips of a between and an
Almost new. I could have sat reading my mail forever.

From the Notepad of Paradise

She told him she would share her book
Her hair was written between the pages
No one was supposed to know what it meant
But her figures boiled in the tracks in the snow
And her teeth were marked around the dialog
Without seeing the crib which hung from a limb
While she moved to the cellar and sang to the lamp
Air surrounded each page as we turned it
One of them was willing to be found in her briefcase
While one chose to remain hidden in the mud
And there up the slope just beyond the old tree
Passing it during no particular time of year
The weather was seasonable but not impossible
His picture limped as it brushed past the pages
She opened and sucked it into her story
Because in some literatures that's how bodies are made
And in others a way to be respectably engaged
Everything was allowed since they barely existed

Compass (a choreography)

The circling plane removed itself from the sky
and settled in a box of liquid.

We knew from her form
she was from out of the country

ground out of glass
till she could glide like an eel over the surface
of the waves.

There were twelve ways of looking at her, one
through a steel cylinder

flooded with supernal light, burped from the underside of a tree.

The mirror reversed itself
her double
burnt on the face on a coin flicked into the air above a lake.

The ivory or the burnished skin
in a bag by the laundry
disguised as an ectoplasmic purse

or aromatic warmer, twirled itself around
runways, felt the interface between

abstraction and moisture.

All day long we were down by the projector. We were by the broken
reactor
copying ourselves into the air, or the car.

All day long the bridge
to tomorrow hurt, the way the cables swept underground.

The copy machine
had reduced itself
to a slide show, so that the first feature was

"why are we here?" or "silver crackers, anyone?"

By the time we got control over the rest of our lives, the reel had

become a sickle over the city.

Her emblem had been awake, had redone our
shopping malls,
mauled us as we slept

in a circle, centered around our teeth,
redistributed
casually, into the next sentence,

or the next century, or something like that.

And screeched like a bell fallen from its joist
sliding down along
the hypotenuse of the roof. She spent

all day trying
to fix us, but then flew to another city.

She spent all afternoon trying to fix us, but remembered
the arc of the compass
turning above our absence of bodies.

A Basket of Fruit

Like gray snow coming in off the desert
Your thoughts smell of sea salt and ivory

Wind rattling your mailbox out of the earth
Scattering your name over the field

As if an idea had fled from a stockpile
Of wishes and lips opened to spread

The invisible. A thought in a cup
Or a thimble roasting on a lead brazier

While heat vanishes faster than it swells
Has got a mind on itself and an eye

On the dinner bell, fading in from
An apparition of voices drenched

In their own tenacity. How to forgo
The dispersal borne out of the hand

Writing itself on a wall while it waits
For the other half to answer. The you

That pluralizes itself sits back down
On a single chair and frets the deletion

It sinks and stumbles towards, longing
To repeat and recognize its contours.

A SMALL BOOK OF EARLY WISHES

What is the far
What is the distance saying?
What is the tar across the sky
what is the advertisement saying
what is the empty tissue dispenser saying about
what is the journey's name?
Did they say it had sound?
Did they say it had a sound its own?
Why is the sun white?
Why is the other green?
Why is the flag (a flutter)?
How about those parentheses—
are they a bickering among the branches
while the night drinks up the trees?
Why when the sun's been down
only a second, or a week or so
why when it's often raining?
When was it
      has it
        does it
last heard unfurling in the fog
the resemblances we can't seem to tame?
What does the angle want?
Where is it that the shadow seeks?
Does it have a loudness?
Does it have a voice?
Is there more in the beam of the inter-
                    seaming
           a quest for one
      or division between—
how is it that your kisses bruise?

How is it that night gets in?
Where had we drawn these lines?
What is the sentence for?
What is this sentence forming?

DROP SCENES

If I knew what I meant when I said
there will be entertainment

Bricks laying bricks laying bricks

with all the sex of a thesis
scribed in the blue on the back of your hand

Why don't you take this river from me

the confluence of fact from my fax hole
so I can spy somewhere else without flying

down the aisles along the inside of a shell

—movie theater with no sound
but a blood-rush through hollowed-out ears

Though by ten feet from the peak of violence

the hum becomes dialog
cough syrup, ergot and electric fences

designed to protect the supermarket
from shedding

its three tears: one for each matchstick

dampened along fire exits and air vents
while the players smoke in refrigeration.

We curved around the center arcing
in a cream of theory fizz

unfortunate as love the man
who walked the perimeter of the zoo

waiting for a waitress from an undecided past. It added up
to not more than an ego boost

per hour, nervous-wreck machine

as even lawless she with the misty
locks undid his personality multiplex

looped through hands of devilishly uppity primal
matter scooped
out of the dashboard radio

at very little volume. These were tastes they made
of seizing on the simplicities—

pleasures of the bedroom program
readout which they welcomed, as they

pushed away the red and homely syntax
the fragrance was finished with unless

I was drunk already when you called, your sweaty

faces dripping, crying when I grabbed them from a wind
barking voicelessly at the dogs next door.

They listened too long, lying beside the edge
of a blotched legal pad. Planned to lever

up a satellite, and join together, hoping
to get back home. But night shifted to a zoological

zone, and the wind retreated up something's
back end. As for me, I tried tying my heads and hands

in knots, though I couldn't figure out how to undo it.
Morning came around earlier than usual,

surpassing any order I'd known. Without flying off
the handle at the several witnesses on

the windowsill I climbed my hair
toward their sacred shapes, and dove into the pool.

Please explain: tired of the baldness leaning
between the gray and green we call a chasm

People think they're made of blinking eyes
but more than air comes between us. Shift

the melody this way, the quake has gone
through the broom closet and is out on the drive

I wish we were something simpler
but the windows have a history, a showing

unequaled on this floor. Best to go
up to the seventeenth where mice are building

a city of glass and ice—numerological
interpretations of the top-forty. All else is "story"

But what do you mean by beauty
The king's been dead an hour or more
Hunting down his proxy paramour

No we haven't established any laws
or personal details. I squid you
Touch-touch the oven's off

The same with this conditioner I'm afraid
Not designed for such rugged commercial acting we were made of swirls
and other reductive miniseries-stunts

the way the cloud gathered in the wheelbarrow and we
tipped over; in a punch and scratch circus
where all our friends the annuals ignited

the flame wistful, hopeful
the way the "end of things" found
their entelechy for an hour. Done with

their cloaks covered with thorns, they made their way
movie-like coming in pink sheets
swollen angles a little blood in their "doing-there."

AN ECONOMY CAN REMEMBER US

Seminar

I was very anxious about it and then there was sand
In the opening between his teeth. Not one of us
Would step closer to the hole. Not one of us would
Step closer to the microphone. He spoke through
His teeth, emitting a hissing sound, a different species
Or perhaps no species, but an outside category. That
Is why I felt it was a safe bet. No one noticed when
He mentioned certain words they fell into a reverie
But I felt it, though that may have been subjective. He
Opened his mouth and the words fell out. They
Fell to the floor and disappeared in the sand. Its teeth
Then would grind loudly as if chewing on large bones
And no one noticed that either. It was an impossible
Situation. We were learning how to sell ourselves to
Others and only then would we sell the product line.
Our customers, the public, political allies, family pets
Small children. We were offering them a service and
That was the subject. With the right kind of mission
Statement. The letters and ideas, and then the sound
Of the sentence coming off his lips as he bit into our
Misconceptions. We really knew nothing about it. I
Felt a certain attraction to his ideas, moving around
In my head like a bag of potato chips. It sang in me.

Seventeen

1. An evening out at the circus

2. The train pulling in and out

3. Questions answering themselves silently

4. Isn't that what night is for

5. A trash receptacle in a labyrinth

6. A circle dancing squares

7. To remind you of a well-greased reflex

8. Your check that's bounced

9. And has continued to ask

10. Though perhaps all of our friends are

11. Nomadic peoples from the past

12. A movement never ending

13. Infiltrates and breaks

14. As if praying to ourselves was a sin

15. Or an economy can remember us

16. Oblique circles of days matching the moon

17. A circle is the center of itself

Dude Descending Bookcase

Thus where you were in the sentence
Or paper bag a page climbing up along
The row of boxes toward the back
Of a storage room in a building of glass
In a car along the river as the bridge
Rises out of the water and into the night sky

In a paragraph made of mud and weeds
Bonded together so the rain won't get in
In a sky of glass in the lobby
Of a building in the center of the word for *go*

Or *haven't yet* a word one never thinks of
Lastly trying to steal a world from its safe
Pressurized cabin as it enters the ozone
Page of the atmosphere accelerating toward
The speed of sound or the speed of popcorn

Burning on the stove before the house goes up
The wind in the window starting to rise
In creeping degrees of warmth that turns
The key in the fence the key in the key in it

THIS DREAMING DEMON

This sentence is used to kill off
All those extra transactions

You've found you made
Somewhere along the line between

Your seedling days and here
It begins the process; you can

Watch it molt, watch it spend
Time with its feral self

Splitting along the rift of
The ribosome, dropping a piece

A sparkling particle or two
Until the network comes to void

And any thought you may
Have had replaces itself

With rain falling; snow perhaps
Or the rising chutes of dandelion

Milkweed, that enviable lightness
Now a part of your step

And all the directions it can take;
This sentence doesn't do

Anything by itself, of course
It is not even a semblance

Nor is it a breath or breadth
Of stone overhanging where you

Might duck to avoid
A hailstorm, like some other

Conveyance may have tried
Or done if you were listening

In your particular crouch
Or fighting stance; one movement

Followed by another is how
We start; first the eyes, then

The tongue, hidden back in
The throat, then the eyes again

And finally the body mute
With its heavy weaponry

The tepid losses it seems
To make as it passes for words

Briefly but so much that it might
Be treated so, its syntax

Of standing and being heard
But then the unrecoverable pieces

Bulging out of the trellis walls.

The Ordering Of Numbers

They rise up in my throat
            only to be swallowed
                        disappear in braids
strands of disaggregation

floating undifferentiated body noise.

I know if every third is odd
                        there has been some mistake
since each has a name
            a propensity.
                        Five

for instance, tends to bully

but I'm beginning

to understand
            him more. It's when there are more *fives*

        than *fours* or *sixes*, in a sequence

that you have to worry. *Threes*

can be a problem as well, and unless

they are surrounded by *fours* and *twos*
                        cause various irritations
and rashes

as they continue to replicate themselves.

The even numbers are the protectors—they

are the police.
                    This is what we learned

when we were very young:

                    the odd numbers couldn't be trusted.

When I was picked on
                    it was an even number
that came to my rescue

a *formidable, sportsman*-like
                    *good*fellow.

Many of the odds, in turn, grew up

to be policemen.
                    I, myself, was odd

although harmless

until now
            with *one*

        and *negative one*

                    wrestling with my feet
                    and hands—when

nobody knows for sure.

THATCHED SCREEN

The sentence is pure energy
No idea like dried blood lies
In its inscription
But a wondering: how did we
Emerge concurrently
This abuse and abuser of tongues
A perversion which subverts
The culprit in the act
Makes his mischief ornamental
In some ways benign
Deader than straw
Made into a summer hat
While out of its mouth comes
A hollow sound
Flashlight tracings along
The borders of a city torn down
Not long after you arrived
A single cell in a wilderness of otherness

ANY LIGHT IN THE SKY

As the moon squashes against the horizon

Characters crawl out of their words

A precipitous climb toward avalanche

Moon and horizon singing to each other

To imagine a chest of drawers

Filled with their lines

Trying in vain to manage themselves

They pile up their lives in thinking

There's a sound without the grinding of hours

Any light in the sky will tell you

This thing derived from

Consternation is liberating

In the end

As the end comes without cause

THE NUMBERS

Glad to see you're coming to the particle accelerator.

Notice that we've named it after you; and all your parts

And zoological extremities have come out to witness this alignment.

Comb your hair what's left of it after the leakage. Being

Cloud makes the maintenance of follicles a difficulty, but

In spirit you are still a radiant creature.

Listing facts by these gradients is a wonderful idea.

You haven't gone off flat or missing yet.

Let all the prize pigs parade inside you.

Literature as Equipment for Living

The reason the door opens and closes
It says. It says, initiate of time
You have run out of numbers, yet there are
Still moments aside to haunt or pierce you.
But no average day; days are not cobbled
Of averages, though to notice like
And not like, helps to raise the city wall.
The door slams or drifts open; it's as if
There was a muscle in my mind, the man
Says, the pink spider who believes it is
A man believes it's said. But there is yet
No song, and there are no names for flowers.
It's as if there was a muscle in our mind
Cramping as the wind moves the door, moves
The mind back another quarter inch. *We*
Says the spider, referring to itself.
And the door says it's me, and draws nines.

SEPTEMBER VARIATIONS

1.

Sun sets over the eastern blank
Fill in the remainder where
The square lacks least
Lacks leaks. We are a bubble coming
in over the west. Our geography
is neutral, catacombed. Inside
our separateness drenched angels
of division go, ideologies blurred.
Sun shreds you to dreads and makes
them part of a party. Let's get in
on the rest. The rest of guts and gets.
The startled watchman. He sparkles
in the crusted cavalcades

2.

Or so you have the irritant
in your eye—so sharp
it's warming. The final. You.
Marching with vapor hammers
we sway. Bend buttresses.
Shards of concrete surround
my clothes. The air. The
final sentence in a book
of gloves. The skin removed
as the gloves are drawn.
Hands found neatly bound
in a mound of debris. We
took them as a souvenir
to a place made out of wind
and smoke. There was a fire
in the elevator and we
stomped it. Windows changing
shape, form reinventing every-
body was happy. Everyb-
ody in the curve. Around corners
piles of books smoldering
And the warmth provided thus

3.

Never say never. Never say today was
If you'd really like to gain access—your
burning thoughts—chew immediately
The sound of light entering the square
The descriptive feelings abstracting
your senses. This is the meant
and toneless vent of night. Night
in the sentence, as when the syntax
distributes the things as they are
gives up. The work of the world
bound easily, spun lazily around
a freckle in the dirt. We might think
we flood the hall with operatic
rosebuds, but see toy soldiers
milking toy sheep and urinating
on the plaza. The wreckage rising
in stone and steel like a plaintiff
forgetting his amnesia. Absolving
with a movie and a warm milk
a freckle heated in the microwave.
Eyes hanging out to dry. Flooding
Windows. Patch this dream with stars.

4.

As is the fashion. As is. Aziz
and Hamlet alone together
on the square. Cab drivers
and infantry men. Sailors
squandering their money. Truck
drivers on the plaza, the
plaza buckling up. Aziz
biting into his ham sandwich
Not one honey trader. Random
axe in Hamlet's hand his eyes
staring off, confused with
themselves, confused with seeing
What word can be used
to describe this this this moving
this gesturing around the way
the outer world describes the inner
somewhat striptease. Aziz
sneezes into Hamlet's handkerchief
as Hamlet loses sense of himself
The motion picture steps in. Closer
but the narrating voice hisses
to a halt. The skies burp. Aziz
and Hamlet are covered with
each other's lunch. Freeze frame

5.

A daring glister portends and a seizure
climbs up the banister ambidextrously

Or so the Manhattan skyline preambles
back and forth against the gray till splitting

its bandages it blends in dearly with itself
a dog or pile of rocks broken across its face

CONVENIENCE STRUGGLES

Inscription under the Bridge

We brought them to the snow
Not what the conscious mind does

But the elastic band
Around your wallet

Called me into the room
There was a name and a day for it

Soldiers standing sentry

These screechings cannot be thought

Days' Treasury

These tender elements refuel the ship
for now's knotty discovery. How would you
like to take a bath in it while morning
has you tying the last of your shoes. By the printing
press but in half the time. The yellowing
of the leather in your room is disasterless
but not fruitless. There is a blue umbrella
over a purple owl whose name is written on a white wall
behind a cart of melons and pamphlets
or manifestos. The letters are so faded even the owl
can barely see them without its special glasses
made of forgetfulness and austerity. It is raining
on the roof but not the patio. An oud player breaks in
and removes his shoes made of his most recent
compositions, but the owl doesn't hear.
He pretends it is bazooki music instead of himself.

Horses (a fable)

The goal of the commission was to get as many
of the *settled* out on vacation
as often as possible, to places like *Bedlam*
Sodom, or *Deconstruction*. It didn't really matter
where, as long as their threads
of hibernation were cut, and as new beings
were allowed a variety of
novel rhythms and strategies
for reading and interpretation.
This, of course, was not what they had wanted at all
having set foot
into deep mud ages ago, and sunk
until the suction was something almost sexual.
So when the laws were passed
and the commissioners began to tie ropes and straps
to their wrists, to pull them out
of the ooze, they complained
and ranted about political oppression. The horses, whose
strength and will were enlisted to be used
for yanking and heaving
were wounded by their guilt of association. So they
began to mistrust the commission,
and decided to start up their own party. They felt
that the ultimate freedom
was the freedom to choose, either the worst situation
or at least the least opportune:
it was possible that what the people
had really wanted and needed
(though they fumed constantly
about feeling stuck) was their seemingly erotic footing
at the very base of their existence. It was

with this realization that the horses
had decided that the enabling power
had become too sophisticated and dangerous
that it was far better and safer
to experience life in wordless immediacy
than with the scheme of signification that the others
chose to continue dreaming.
Once of noble lineage, they had soon
become the new underclass, though
this they never understood, having
disciplined themselves to resist articulation.

Noise Level

Technically this could be truce, but who
could ever judge. Judge not, said the pharaoh's
daughter, but she hadn't had a piece yet.

True to form she was a worrier, with an even
longer neck. Marksmen spent time shooting
inside her head. They didn't know it was possible.

But as students we remained within her eyes.
She took the silver out of the cup to show us
the difference between the back and side.

The quiet was blotting out the nose level
above her noise. The pharaoh sat on his throne
counting the mishaps he loaded in a revolver.

His daughter was neat as a pin, and decorated
with feathers and mirrored chips sewn into
her gown. She negotiated with her broken being.

I walked through the front door with the silver
bullets in my head. The pharaoh reminded me
that I should take off my shoes. She was a virgin.

I was mannequined for a while, made into pencil
rubbers until she saved me. I lived with her
in a wall safe toward the back of her studio.

We were still waiting for someone to cut the cake.
A roundish fellow with a green wig came and
invited us to a red party. We were left on a stair.

But our friend from the infirmary was dressed in
the tension he had absorbed on his way over.
He was wearing gray negligence and regulated hair.

We had to cut him a piece of the evidence; it was
the pharaoh's mistake. Everybody ground
themselves into the mirror and went nowhere.

Some -Ologies of Identification

Some kind of science was running out of her mouth.
She was the shape of a bullet and came through
a tropical storm to meet you here. What was

her device and what her advisement? The singular way
she stored her angularities in the movement
of her head. This was the weapon of the sort tongues

use when wrestling with themselves, the administrators
within themselves, who barrel through walls
of glass with uranium ore and bricks of blood.

As daughter to the pharaoh she was responsible
for laying the groundwork, lying on the ground
working her clothes off, for divining the substance

held by a spout in the ground, for grinding
down with a cyclotron's balm, until the surface
corrupts and you are no longer a virtuous clown.

You are a neighborhood or state or autocrat or film
over the teeth of the army, dog over the teeth
climbing over its teeth into a sewage plant or bar.

And though she is truly as weaponless as you are
your waterwheel is ever hunger in her current
and you are the lemonade she spills in your eyes.

ROMAN HOLIDAY

The song reminds itself it must have a singer
While the dance collects its baggage
And clowns dig latrines for the infantry moving in
Down the street. Diogenes quickly shits
Into the air and rolls in his bowl
Up the hill around the schoolyard, where he will
Hide himself among the training
Gear and bleachers by the football field.

He has become *operatively transparent* according to
A textbook on espionage and invasive
Cultural surgery, but he is reminded by the song
How the set is changed if the decisions
To defoliate the grounds has been ignored or

Forgotten. The song reminds itself again about
The new relationship that's heckling into being
As the soldiers reposition themselves along
The road with shovels and trumpet mutes
And the song slides down the hill at the end
Of a row of trees and has aural sex with itself.

An Encounter with Philosophy 1

The natural spirit reclines,
saunters, in a kind of jellied motion
brought about by figuring out how high
the army pasted their idea additions

A blonde in a capsule grew seven
heads green and an evening
out among the tweed effects for launching
made wandering hair stuck to the ceiling

For without her golden buckle
there would be less of us to transpose
into a logical music. No ear whacks
to instigate more than enough load carryon

Overdeveloped yesterday
where she showed you ill effects
of landing why not house the candles in wax
if that was what they were. All day

There were forty thieves, and they drank from the same glass as the woman came down the staircase. Half of them were wearing blonde wigs, while the rest were hidden by tufts of white smoke on a pale silver plate. It was photographed by a man without any arms. They had been cut off in production to make room for the explanatory text. It was in an article called *An Encounter With Philosophy* (or *The Red Queen's Last Pituitary*). Few people had come because of the weather, but I heard it was quite a party. We got lost in the vestibule, where there had been a number of chilling views, and lather for everyone, and we crawled on our paws, dismantling the speakers. Nobody spoke Hindi, and nobody smoked Houdini, but there was a cake out in the hail. Who did it? It was Friday. We didn't have to go to work in the morning. It was Tuesday. Several of us had to blow our noses at once. There was an echo. There was a vibration and reverberation. A train pulled into the station. We were put back into the terrarium, and somebody laughed. The TV went blank. You were lost in your electric blanket.

Romance and Fountain

:Don't want a Martini I'm wearing a tunic
Give it to the have-gots at the other edge
Of the party. Usual Cartesian responses. No

:The universe is not square. A broiled Brooklyn
Habit arc accents subtly without a dash—
But would be believable not in this kingdom

:Excuse me please the universe is coming
Over the next few responses are coming
For dinner: halving the moons in mid-drifts

:Your argument is linguini. Window clean
Sorbet of twenty-first century five & dime
Has the clearest urinals in Jersey City. PS:

The Inenviable

The sun rises and the beach is scoured
With trebly lines. People forget and enter
Through numerous lacerations believing

That it strengthens their connection to
The numinous in them. Lines like the once
Eroticized fingernail traces

In the frost of a back seat window. Nature
It is said, leaves its incomplete insignia
Repeatedly, forcing guesses. Where

The undulations of the sea meet the
Crenellations of the sand. Where to go
From here? Only desire guesses it can

Say so. Whispering its silent agency
Its secret police everywhere impossible
To detect. Singing wind over the grain.

CONVENIENCE STRUGGLES

After being admitted out into the rain
He found his camera had an aperture
And in that aperture was an abyss
Did the abyss think with him when he thought
Of it, did it sing to him with its silky lines
Like a mouth torn off the sky at night
And implanted in the maturity of his knowing
In its paranoid purity, its simplicity
Lining the nest with stones, gold seat with deadfall
And leaves? It was convenient to say so
To think so murdered the self one was not
The idea in the first place, meaning it was different

POMPEII

I kissed her hand, bent several fingers earthward,
hoping to unwind her thread of waist around my wrist.
But there was a partially erased venture-capitalist
smeared along the doorjamb. Why was he in the forest to begin with?
And why was he asking us all of those questions, unheedingly,
as if... The trash compactor grabbed his head and made a lot of noise.
What's it we'd just said about the opening of the mail,
that sleepy rite, all those buckets and drawers swinging into view,
the unzippering, unstapling of the wound? He said he sped through stop signs,
shopping malls, housed a direct mail counter-flow in the rear
compartment of our belatedness, where the working week ends
and dissolves the toy inside our atrophy, or the moon
in someone's ornate shaving case. His radial distributive powers,
and audacious supply of offal smiles, revived our sense of melding,
scribbled along the edge of a map we had sectioned off
and made suctions of. We hadn't known we were environmentalists.
So my head was made into a tool for hammering nails into a tree.
She preferred it that way. But on the other hand it is a spy,
every tooth locked in a helpful grip. The dog refused and ate plaster.
The mailbox collapsed. We all wore pine-wood ur-dresses
and crawled on the floor, sniffing for facts we had forgotten. We watched
as Tuesday strayed out of her convertible, drowned Saturday
until the uneven layers of mint & cheese collected in the furrow
between her breasts. I ordered, reordered, and over-ordered the clowns
for our sympathy parade so they'd come by broken up in little overalls
and silver jackets, hair stuck between their teeth after lapping
at each other's violins for several hours after jury duty.
But back in his Bermuda shorts he met a guest, had stuffed a tracing
of the dark side of her mind, written on a strip of skin
he'd peeled off her sunburned butt that afternoon while
blasting off in reverse, landing-gear fully extended into the brush.

DINNER IN LE JARDIN DURÉE

What do you think of this moment
That was more than dirty clowns ago
And the picture on the cheese wedge or on the jet
Where was your wallet when you last saw it?
Hours and hours ago, when I was forgetting
And the sequence, those forty frames
Fell out with your money
Flew down the street, caught in trees
Lost in thought, he held his fork
Limbs wrapped a ribcage around his mouth
While she followed the sentence
To the end of the sentence, to the end
Of the honey. You were handsome
When you were young. She said.
She heard, she said. To the hub of the sound
A moment in the trees. Time slowed to a murmur.
Glowering within the sap of leaves
With the recording equipment
Still in the boxes and plastic sleeves
A moment took over thirty minutes
He stared off and forgot her name
Wine drops on the edam and surrounding areas
An hour later she searched his pockets
There was no record of this ever happening
She laughed. She pulled the trigger
The scent tore at his eyes and he paid the tab

Warm Air

The time to salute the Caesars is over
Now that you've blown our cover
And the foreground is rent in abstraction

Hail beneficiaries of lucrative trusts
The heat transmitted from your body
Is a weather system of its own

And that is how our sadness reaches you
We build these tunnels and domes
Filling them with vague geometric chill

INVASION VARIATIONS

I was lying in bed, trying to get back to sleep when suddenly, tap tap... tap tap... I recognized that sound, though it took me a moment, from two or three years ago, when the current super was on hiatus in Brazil. It went on, it seemed, for months, and then stopped unaccountably.

I tore myself out of bed and scurried around the apartment until I could think of what to do, finally grabbing a pot from the stove and placing it on the ground where most of the water seemed to be landing. I moved the old pillows I've been meaning to throw away, and brought three books back onto dryer ground, but alas, poor *Nadja* was soaked through and would never be the same again. At least the *Tractatus* was somewhat intact.

Breton told me the best way to deal with the fact of war was to not talk about it, in that way refuse to participate with its desire to consume all things; but my friend Paul walked offstage, more perplexed than angry, when he found I had erased or distorted his lines. And so, what do I do, sitting here in relative comfort, trying to get the *word* to spin worlds, while the one that is supposedly real, before me, brought to me through a box of light and the talking box, as well as my friends and the people I meet (talking like boxes)—what am I supposed to do about that brutal patch of map where I am told there is a lot of noise, many fleshy, conscious *its*, like this *me* that sits here, as they screech in convulsions, or—in an instant—are coming to an end. What am I supposed to think?

This: lean forward and touch the air: it wasn't for several days you could buy that package: the sweater and the mountain gear: and all across the street, of course: and there was a welcoming party and a big parade.

We walked into a sideshow, or a side street, and came upon a broken mirror. Forget what we called it. We called it *name of dog*. We called it and it came to us after dampening the ground around the rocket launcher. After a while there are others like us, and after lunch they were gone. This year the celebration had gotten very loud and our homes had become mounds we could climb on.

There is a treatment of the text something like midnight, which I had an hour to misconstrue. She snapped like a Venus Flytrap, and immediately we were hurtling over Morocco, in a more or less salvage-quality carpet—unreliable textile, frayed (or perhaps afraid) at the edges. But she sent us along with a collection of bologna sandwiches we were to research until we landed one day in Bangladesh, where George Harrison was having some sort of new electric guitar built out of balsa, and a wood that grows only around the Ganges. That's if we make it through the air strike. Perhaps it's not actually *wood* at all, but something imagined by the dead as they float shrouded and stiff as canoes. Wait, I'll have mine with mustard. Maybe we could get a new one before we start off again.

The news arrived at the crime scene, just before the party started. It came wearing a plaid ascot and a daffodil through a button hole, but no one was allowed to decipher it. He tried to break a sailor's neck, but the sailor just went ahead sawing away at the furniture. Soon there were two of everything, and the next thing we knew it was time for breakfast. Or nearly. We still had a half-gallon of vodka to finish, and a pint of paint thinner we had been using to remove our clothing, or the lines we had drawn beneath out eyes while we were still awake. But the news was still at it, though it had changed into a woman in a slight bathing suit, covered from head to toe with black & blue marks. Finally, I found out how to work the remote.

*

The chief imbecile recorded himself falling off the stage. We were astounded by his recreational abilities. Where did he put the microphone and where was he flying to? I had coughed up a piece of burnt linoleum after he had given me the go-ahead. What stage of life was that? It seemed like a miracle that he swallowed the audience—I remember living in an altered state for several years after that, something like Wyoming, but with less fuss over the antelope. I don't remember what I had eaten but it disintegrated my esophagus. Whole villages made of mayonnaise, living quickly, rotting in the sun. At his instructions we catapulted ourselves against the wall behind the curtain, ran like broken eggs down-field toward the goal line, where we were each handed a number two pencil and a book of boxes.

This summer unrest: but why winter again, just like that? We are moving with the speed of CNN through manifestoes of circuitry. Electrical impulses gouge my brain, but I know how to enjoy it. I snake my board through the refuse of countless New York Times book reviews to meet you here, where you wipe the spittle off your dolls and building blocks, preparing for a nose bleed.

Who's been playing with the air again? Sharp hot moments, three of my friends already melted, but they were only made out of plastic. I wonder if the moon is made out of stuff like this. The pavement so broken up over last night's party. Hard to tell from your facelift. Let's drip wax over everything. I've got some aroma therapy candles. You're not going to be using that eye anymore, are you? Everything's dropped back to two dimensions. Take what you need, and take a little more. I heard there was a formula for making lots of money. Take your fingers out of your ears. You won't be needing them anymore.

IN THE ABSENCE OF A LAMP

Elizabethan Pamphlet

The law of the jungle says all things will cannibalize themselves
All things will fall into disuse

Side by side we have a red chart
And a blue chart. We no longer have any need for a green chart

A red cart and a blue cart. The oily cart
Still moves the other has lost its wheels

We no longer use the words of the seamstress and her mistress
Though there are stress marks on this one

Its wheels are bent and it's no longer any good for carrying
Signals to and from the television. The law of the jungle

Says a bent antenna is better than none. It says
How can I help you Please will you go now I have a headache

The seamstress biting the blue thread returns to her 17th century
Disappears in the padded pattern of her mistress

The size of the jungle is proportionate to the law that surrounds it
And the silence it evokes when the red light flashes

The Problem with Autopoly

The void came through her window and sacked out on
the sofa while the image of a nightingale flew across
the screen. It wasn't a matter of helplessness, but the special
potion concocted in order for her to realize the depth of
the disaster: Sunday morning the mechanical shark
demolished the bathtub, and then Tuesday a voice called
from within her sequin hat, admitting responsibility for
some of the unseemly acts accompanying the revolution.
The void stood up and exclaimed a while, telling how
it fed ducks to the river, early one summer, while waiting
for a postcard from a lover who had moved to Brazil.
The secret of the succession, it said, owed everything
to the balance between two forces attributed to ocular motor
functions and the way the sun splashes into the mountains
before tumbling onto the coast and everything in between.
That's presumably where the war had broken out, had cultivated
and grown to prosper, until it was a mature and fickle being
ripe for waste, and at a marriageable age. But the ducks
came equipped with their version of the conflict, resembling
a treatise on chess tourneys more than an allergic fascination
with smoke, hot flashes and gore, and since they had fluency
with several languages, made a much stronger impression
than did the rotisserie chickens, which didn't say a word
in any language, but either sat silently in an icy tray
or spun around like sick prom queens before they passed
out and puked on everyone, lurching out onto the beach
with the wrong date. She couldn't get her camera out quickly
enough, and soon the ducks had eaten through to the back seat.

UNPACKING

The bull flowers against the brick wall

He is crushed

He is made of mice and eats only the trash
left by the vector of the Victrola

Squares were falling from the ceiling
but they had no dimension

And pretty soon the bull had redesigned itself
into a trailer park of wasps, and small people

made of clay
and the dung of dungbeetles

Surfaces everywhere. Everything about this house
was paper thin, or less

So he went off into the forest to find a maze he knew

Having no dimension meant having to fight
for space, for a volume
of clouds on which ghosts stood

resembled one another, smoked
as streaks of quark and ember filled the container

A name takes no space, but arguing it will

She said *bull*, and he said *I have an aquarium*
like you

The Cracked Case

How was it we had no notion.
We were born awake

started quick by remaining ghosts layering musical tableau

before the glass caved in
got locked in the open around
the perimeter of the station. All this talk

of war and intrigue was only here to remind you
of your natal urge
which was to flood your fingers with red crayons

along the edge of some elevated
calendar
of spring before cramping its desire.

Invisible Mind

Something in the dark was waiting
for you: shadow of a hand or a man—

How can there be a hand wrapped
in shadow in the darkness

when the night needs light
to be afraid. It was his dark suit

Nevermind says the murmur
and a robin singing on a windowsill

This show's got a murder tucked beneath
but we can only hear it swallow us

I seem to lose control of you
the swallow sings to who knows whom

and the absence of a lamp
shining at night atop a crooked elm

The night he seems to lose control of:
the man hid away beneath a scroll

of light as dawn paints coils
disappearing in the evening

The dawn is might. It smells
not sulfur nor wholly of pine

but the breath of itself
its cinemas of corn fields

on their way out of sleeping
the grin of incident signatures

THE MAN INSIDE THE MAN INSIDE

He may argue
if it's imagined it's probably real

Or he might say
this cloud a little over here

the air in it no specific color

but a contact
with the resourcefulness of remorse

It's not real but it better be

we're counting on
its specific height and weight

the way it grinds and shapes the lens
of our approach

Since we seize it with a kind acculturation
dew from the lemon grove

dropping in a pail of postcards
sweetening the mail

Letters which cruise up the spine
arrange themselves the way dust would

on objects not yet specified

This movie advancing like
a shoe in the rain

barking at a mural
in the back of kitchen or pool hall

There had been classes there during
an earlier century

Children learning how to spell
words they would never need

crawling down mine shafts
one idea after another

Faces lit up alphabetical
lit up with the untellable

People who've enjoyed their work

and people folded over lamplight

Trying to hide from
a knowing that is wholly assertive

The Song as Apprehension of the Am

*X*ed off from daylight, the silent hum
Threads thought to thought, note to throat,
Glimmer to glass, sweat, chrome or eye,
Walks with you through street or wood.

It sings for you, though you don't hear it,
Describes the world, images aligned
And measured, one against another,
Casts them back, arranged by sleep.

Sings for you: boulder by brook, tree by street,
Objects to itself when you object to it,
Toils without knowing how hard it works,
Titles itself with your name as you speak.

The Song is the *am* when the *I* is not
(Still lies mute and unassembled),
Draws it together, as the spider knots
Its glutinous spittle in a silk dream.

What's Eating You

We settled in a small crevice
between his cheek and nose.
Nobody knew we were there yet.
Not even after our church bells began to ring
loudly, and we were arguing
shouting in the central square.
His doctors had looked at the bruise,
prodded around where the pain came from.
There was no lesion, but a desire
to move, transmitted along the skin
from where we were sitting.
Our names were Holly Roberts and Delmore Fudd.
In another version we were called viruses
or bacterium,
a company of awkward and barely
intelligible demons—
because we were smaller than gods
or humans (the name calling and accusations!)
We were pugnacious as well,
so with sticks, stones, rubber and vinyl
we built higher.
When our settlement had become a city
our host scratched his eyes out
stumbling around peep shows, ravaged lamp posts
learning to see, or to say so.

Out of Another

Crank design industry
will pay us
reasonable
      fuzzy organization

if now we care   in it   the friendly
                          box
by discovering
went
home without   not long

a heart torn decorative

shirt copy bigger

finger
housed
     what
waxed in lack

I grew to seven feet that year
but was cut down
in order to make a better student
Things at the factory
hadn't gone as well as expected
At eight o'clock we reached
the terrain and buried
the boxes in the snow. Very loud.
I thought my mother would
appreciate the petunias more
than the narcissus. We all stood
for the pledge of allegiance, but

when she took them from me
I began to sink and noticed
I was wounded. No one
paid us any mind, replacing
parts of our bodies with
inanimate objects became an
acceptable mode of sexuality.

Activation Warning: where that shirt.

He was only being mystical

air strikes and cruise missile attacks
end of his offensive critics in Kosovo

but the sixteen Haitian lions sued
meaning chiefs
and other equipment
when their allies would move
would contribute
but officials
you say the classics are the things to breed with
when dulled and disconnected
can once again remember
that cleared away feeling
trick as well as laughter
violent and habitual distortions
which are they?
in the (voices loop) throughout my
water ever happened
to mine conscience-
ness

Lament (sonnet):

SO: (once upon a time there used to be
an advent garter—throat id wuz the one
and only one that we could) END OF LINE THREE
a head cold tried to make an END OF fun

FATAL ERROR("that cleared-away feeling")

They dragged me in from the school yard
just behind the girls' gym door
after a curtain of yellow TV snow
fell through me wrapped a cocoon
around the school yard dragged me
in just after the curtain fellow wrapped
the girls gym door around my snow
forcing me behind my knees the girls
fell through me my friends the schoolyard

Lament (folk ballad):

Time in prison
Free to do as I please
With expert derision
Five of us streak chalk across our foreheads
(something sneezes)
Bang them—

Do it or I'll tell mother on you.
(*I grew to seven feet that year*)

An Acceptable Mode of Sexuality;

He wore his diaper to the opera
but no one knew what *he* was designating
or whether he was only hesitating
to admit that he was nothing—only a
design, a shadow on the wall between
the window and the charcoal grill. He took
the chalk and streaked it on his fresh-wiped book,
implored the node to open, felt obscene
and happy. Then when he remembered he
was one in five, he led them onto war
to prove that he could marry, bonded
to a molecule or trusting family—
Well...? is that you out there? The other four?
The ward was pitched, and he was reprimanded.

So they made another one out of all the other ones

He was only being mystical: boxes in the snow

So they made: *Between the window and the charcoal grill*

I am free to do as I please

Where that shirt

That *cleared-away* feeling

Do it now or I'll tell mother on you

So they made another one out of all the other ones

Self-styled Ceiling

My name was "when spaceships landed"
But more recently people have come to know
Me as "the situation will never be the same"
Ideas have filled my heads for years, and I have become
Somewhat of a hive. I have become a recluse
Since in this world the other is a picture
And all its talk and all its doing, running about
Moving from square to square, pixel to pixel
Is preemptive fumbling, is me watching from inside
Which is why they sent me. Not for nothing
They sent me for committing errors—not crimes
They sent me flowers and gift certificates
I was in the movies when they sent this body
So I could smell it, taste it, not like I can now

Move over—of course I lie to you. There's no place
To go no place to be except this languid saying
Long march which never quite began or ended
But spreads across the papered geography
The way water evaporates. I rode the shaft
Through every brain in my body
But nothing happened. I found myself amid
Ecclesiastical nurses trying to fall down
The chute into the garbage bin of redemptive sin.
I tried to mix with them but they couldn't see me.
No one knew my name so I went on a budget.
I tore hunks out of their faces until they
Looked more like the kinds of arguments
I needed. My name is solar baby. Or wing wing wing.

PLAN FOR A BROKEN BOWL

"It may be that the deep necessity of art
is the examination of self-deception."
—Robert Motherwell

Diagram A

Dead grass and some lipstick outlining
the spot where a tree had fallen.

It wasn't just a spot.

The area spread out an influence
a news on the body's flung dalliance.

Dense collections of dots
on the face of the photograph.

A word written in reverse, perverting
the seams

where the thread, the
spiraling wire tells in redundant

script, looping in roots and the blades
of grass that have lived, stained

the page, died and lived again.

So with these markings
on our faces, intuitions, private

matter in a memory or dream.

Shadow without an object or a sun,
emitting its own light.

I have eaten these things
I have known their texture on my tongue

Inaudible sound as the air feels
when moisture and light inseparably

soothe the wound made by warbling
made by bad song, the chewed up breath

Diagram B

You helped construct a maze known as
Put your money where your mouth is
Though most mouths, they say, are too
Unclean to taste money in its pure form
Spraying out of the wells in apostrophe
On our homes, its starlight concentrate
Cool as the night it falls out of

Vacuous sky, the unrecoverable
Voice spraying awake the vital organs
Money as battle hammer or salve
Free of numerological trappings
Extracted from paper and machinery
As the ardor of brute chance, sensations
Of movement without movement to sense

The money in you that scratches your head
When you crash into a wall you thought
Was a door, sighing through keyholes
Refracted in droplets of dense color
Unfamiliar or forgotten familiar, reactions
Of instants long ago, pleasures so deeply quick
You've lost your way to how it made you

Diagram C

The sun opens its mouth over the bridge
And warms the eastern sky above
The ocean, which is mottled from
Talking to itself so much while we slept

Though this is only a way of speaking.
The sun opens up in physical moments
Through sensory mechanics congealed
And overfed, the eastern sky over

Memory and its way of saying
And arranging. And to talk about how
It is always an opera, monkey singing
Reason as another monkey song

Talking to itself so much while we slept
Filling form with hums and squawks
While I was trying to say, he was trying
To say what I set out to say without

Digression, analogy; but even setting out
Is the sky over the ocean, and the unknown
Stepping out to tease the unthought out
Of the other, the thing recorded or wrought

Only accidentally may chance to notice
Something in the invented record of what.

Diagram D

The running: whatever it may provide it stands in question
may invent and venture
learning under catastrophic
what in times the shallow pools

Reflected upward
having in itself no light and no question
spanning pages
lines appear and unevenly there are lakes upon

The world it sees
and entanglements
spanning questions meant as mist

What about this reflex of the door open to silence
and projection, science
of these bar chords
and their bite
what about violins at pavilions

Unsheathed layers of the mouth without a voice
considered the something or other
pushing pins in its balloons

Pins into these seconds are tones striking

One eye at a time, blurred to watch what lines
will help or survive
crystalline operations of dream work.

And sleep them into tools

Mouthfuls of sameness alive and vociferous forest
the trees warm coil
what may or not hope or believe

Diagram E

Pay attention: this here: dirt on a page: dirt under nails: nails maybe words: page of lines: page of holes: along the edge: lines and holes going out: a search for intent.

It wants to impress you: it wants to press even on itself: what starts: whatever the excitement: outward from life: that is thought: that is not: and where these knives cross.

A kiss through a pane of glass: a kiss on a mirror: mirror by eyes extended: as a way to imagine: waiting by the telephone: and who is it not but the what of your voice: by the extensions: our living through: each word armed or fingered: reaching for you through the book: the blue monitor: sound of helicopters brushing a window: you in earnest: you are right here: and the other you we still look for: somehow enacted by: the unreal incomplete somewhat: impetus of the actual.

DIAGRAM F

Off to work and there he finds a mouth
Of stone filled with cigarette butts

And cracked teeth, dead roaches
And old shoes, lottery tickets, papers

Stuffed in an envelope covered
By stanzas, diagrams

Of organ experience, the way
The body may have functioned

Under other evolutions.
The mouth is silent but hears its

Agonizing in the negative range
Below the line in the darkness of sound.

And it is toward the resolution
Of that song that it works in sparks

Diagram G

Is it possible to be a better sample?
Is it something one should attend to?
Organizations exist, supporting varieties of growth
spiritual or neuro-physical modalities
though deflation's float parades in full regalia
crying for a breath mint. More to overcome
than these rigged up pinions coalescing
chemistry and symbology never meeting
but fondling each other's work with rubber gloves

This region of tiniest knowledge
forcing a smile after you praise Jove
bring the warmth to your chest; we are both
missing something what you call miraculous
perhaps system dynamics, but neither
clues further interrogation of phenomena
will only cause more movies to be made

Hammered together with rifle and pile driver.
Choose your weapons. Next space flight
is affordable real estate, onto your sidewalk
the Times to your doorstep. Cover photos tip
dozens of rare flowers to soften the lost
invented another day and its contingencies

A textile woven in the dark: each flash points out
another pattern in its weave, until even
the eye mistrusts and wishes it could sing
the breath's wishes it could hear. Together
they body and form sentences, analyze
and paint, or is that the minerals themselves
deposited on the walls of the old canal?

Diagram H

I am the monster at the end of this book
and you are the extra strength pain reliever

All is functioning cleanly, all parameters
are set and the camera zooms safely

from a distance. I'm supposed to pledge
accountable, yes, but words flap from

my mouth in growls and clicks you say
need to construe, an opposable thumb

Until now I was only an observer
but I've begun to shine, to hum

and smoke. Flames lick my many
windows you imagine I might have

shutters or little cabinets, each one
with a pad and pencil with answers

to each of your questions, fathomless
and unquenchable. Your rubber hammer

on my head to help me sleep at night.
For sleep is what I have come to utter.

Diagram I

I confess to having these thoughts
these recycled tropes. Uncertainties

stream through meshwork before
a projector creating doped up

translocations, and their resulting
tissues are a dry rot protocol

to the standard procedure. Data in
Data out. Data in through the wrong

terrain to another. All the precision,
it took algorithms and soaking in

sensations and catwalks of the abstract
as when one pulls the tooth out

of a book, leaving a simple paragraph
explaining the viscosities of a flash.

I knew the end had come, but only
of one moment and then all others

so I could see what I could not see
behind my eye-frame of a cache.

Diagram J

—for Kambiz Naficy

It was you who told us how you walked
sideways one day down a mountain

Because of those extraordinary
circumstances, you thought that's how

you had to make your descent. You felt
that often similar squeezing through

narrow circuits, spinning to create
the necessary velocity to break

the folds, their order and arrangements
waves of muck made in past memory,

the shape of an eyebrow conformed
to another, more familiar, or the hood

of a car, in which the blur subsides
with its glaze of identity, to walk

that result, to rise sideways, either
or down if one can't tell the difference.

Diagram K

These words hope to fill you for a moment
And if by chance someone knows what was meant
Thinking about other things, asking which color
Were you seeing when you thought of a house?
What shape was the mailbox? The inkblot wore
A yellow dress and saying I am yes
To the fireman to the volunteer farmer
With a daisy in his head. He had a
Fire in his legs and a ladder and a plow
But yellow inkblot never asked him how
He was and that's because, because he wasn't
These wishes of his are what's left over
After a day of nothing and an eyeful of doesn't

Diagram L

Hoisted upon us
with a bang bang crackle
the world is; and is flickering
there beyond the sheets
hanging in the window
attempting to foil the pleasure
a real life as it masticates
the opportunity. This doesn't want
to talk about muck s...
liding along the edge of a river

The banks are closed.

The booming
of their equations
form new faces, opening
a place at hesitation

DIAGRAM M

Nothing is working.

You take your saucer-shaped difficulties to a new angle from which
armies could be sped rising against the effrontery, carrying themselves
about in invisible buckets. But even with that gesture your seams

begin to show the corona colors that mark defeat, and so you must fall
back on who you are, however they burn their way toward return.
A glaring map is all you ever dreamed of, all you believed

you needed to find your way back to a section of the road you may
have never left nor ever seen, though perhaps you are mistaking
the scene of a movie for what you were, or the blessings of ghosts

and demons gathered around your crib for an adventure you
vaguely recall, through the attics or the disappearance
of the present moment. There was a collision of memories

coalescing themselves into something velvet. A man or woman
with wings flew out of a cake perhaps, or you were watching it
on television when they announced the election results. There are

many reasons to want to go away and they have soaked into
the wood grain of your walking staff, its pointed weapon designed
to gore the flesh of clocks, to spin their blood in twists to change time

for all time, asking always from where will that magnetic moment come.

Diagram N

—for Damian VanDenburgh

There was a violin floating in the bay, or was it a buoy marking
a lobster pot? The closer you looked the more the miraculous
burned away for something else. What is really looking when
the mirror's a condition flecked in decals, vapid hearsay?
What do you see when you look at your hand but all of your
memories of that hand, and the rules of stone for the stone
in your hand, if you're lucky enough to be holding a stone,
and not a feather, while under a rout, or a block of wood,
a pen, with its function and dependencies; and all those
knotted interactions among all others that mock up a world
and its drudgery, identity? It doesn't matter that the violin
was not a violin, because you had begun to hear it until a cloud
had come and dropped a shadow over the glare you had been
staring into. It didn't matter that an enemy was not an enemy,
since now he is dead and will never have the opportunity.
Better to imagine a violin bobbing on the waves, even if
in the end the advancing shadows murder magic, reveal
the bobbing cork, the charm shrinking away at plastic foam;
ever asking what it is, and the surface where the water threads,
how each blur holds anxiously a world in place, binds us
to what we do, while we haven't moved a muscle, or an inch.

Diagram O

This may not be the same day anymore
if ever it was
or if days change as eyes open and close
and the sun capriciously skims the sky
according to whim

I just don't know what's up
or underground
my opinions run me
mucky and deeply drugged
on clouded dissipations all around me

Nothing to think but
what I think I am
wrought on fear and want
their streams of cause and each
shaping the other as itself

These thoughts that pock the sky
and think as music
for a moment, making dots
that fill the air, dusty, heavily aromatic
humming in fingertips, quickly edged

Diagram P

You were younger once, and so you will be again, but not until the red
cloud hinders more of yourself sectioning in introjections, the coughs of
splintering other souls imposing on the small island of propriety you call
your forgotten selves; selfhood segmented and reformed with a giant's
enabling power so you can skate across the ice in quick arcs resembling
the demon god's signature. And if the only thing to learn grew out of this
brief rapidity into many falsehoods, then that's the street you grew up on,
folding artificial light onto the horizon until clouds of granite crush it.

But if that's not the direction you want to go, there are other magazines,
fashion statements, aerosol cans filled with baby's breath. There are al-
ways fine lists and tabulations, but no map to follow, only *the voice* heard
now and again, that rickety radio signal you encounter on a mountain
road. The engine whines in low gear, as it sweats and chokes, guzzling for
air. Various sizes and fields of slippery and false memories grumble from
the sewer of your education.

This will begin again and perhaps not, if you let it.

DIAGRAM Q

The silence of the denominator raises its stake
and in the gifted crowd certain thirsts become ideas
to be asked about. What kinds of features have

us standing in observance, what kinds of paths
run like guess-one's-lover's intensified quala
for how the days open bread-like, open

sweeping the entranceway of their cavernous
mouth for your muddy boots to add flavor?
But how many of those and how many of these

should be chosen to strike a balance, and can
that be answered without consulting the sums of
certain magic books, presumably unauthored

readable only in one's dreams, or broken
open in the center of a fruit, its core and
seeds which supposedly represent nothing?

Diagram R

When Leonardo mapped the body he sketched out what he found within the flesh of the dead; when Vedic philosophers did the same they formed topologies of sensation.

Only one course was objective, observing the body as an object, and the other was as subject.

In the second case the body is not defined by how it can be detected by the senses, and their extensions, i.e. arrangements of lenses, but by what its senses can gather or manufacture.

These observers spent time not slicing apart what was left after life had exited, but attending to the only bodies they had subjectively available: their own, and at times the bodies of their lovers.

Eventually they found through mimicry they could approach knowledge of the sensations of others, and then create through confabulation those which could only be imagined in sequences of events called stories, images of the ideal face each subject wished to possess.

It was then that the wish was formed as an idea and a voice would carry one's wish into the air to extend the sensual range of that body as prayer, and as song.

As the wishes grew in complexity they needed greater tabulation or to be arranged in sequences and variations of sounds and their associations with the living.

And so their corpses find their way to the page in what is written, as is here, a wish that can no longer know itself but only sing and search attempting to mend the division its logic wept into the confusion of so many wishes.

Diagram S

I am not a person and neither am I. We are only thoughts which listen to us and then stop. What is this but what's been counted already, eyes riding over the horizon, or stuck in a corner. Where you have gone is talking about the smoke, thin apoplectic haze and hallucinations that learning engenders. Where I see two men carrying a sign someone sees a large bird with man-shaped wings. Where I hear holiday music someone hears a command to kill, ideas whether they be fleeting or fully grown people.

Flesh as thick as where is your meal, if it is an epiphany, as stuffed or only a dream. Thick as wondering always molecular spasms of muscular rigidity and cramp, otherwise sloppily, nonchalant, like the living we do between thoughts by previous actions forming habits. At repossessed, added to itinerary, the daily gambol of reaching and bending over to pick oneself up, and how it becomes its central theme, axiom and style of life, starting always over at the beginning as if a beginning there was and an ideal target to aspire to, so important to have a place to go in the end, having no place to go. And you're sitting in it. This instant the only rapture of eternity you'll ever know. And missing it, missing every moment until it will eventually go. So you have made a science out of thinking there was something else, some other soup sitting on the kitchen stove, so you can stand in it and feel your enlightenment, that flashing above your head and filling you up so you might be the aboveness in a narrative of some complexity. Though there's no above and below, only forces sticking you to the skin of a ball, as it weaves its elliptical script across an undetermined space. Some place other than what you know. Being right where you are. The size of it, the intent something other than what might matter. If scale determines what matters. Can the sky know what the eye can see of it, when the sky is only an idea? Think of it from the sky's point of view. Where would you find yourself? It makes one nervous to ever think of oneself and the sky in the same room. The sky sick with vertigo reaching upward for something beyond it. It has memories of you holding your tongue out and letting it in through your mouth. Raindrops, where do they come from, do we really believe in clouds? I have a ceiling in this room, I am the ceiling of this room, and you are my thoughts. As I am to you.

Diagram T

We may expect a thing to happen and end up seeing it that way even in
our memories, though the light may break now and then over our dream-
ing while awake to keep us from slamming our new SUV into something
much bigger and bolder, be it a tree of several hundred years, or a build-
ing in one town where it hadn't been in another, though they were other-
wise as similar as the back of playing cards drawn from the same deck,
spread around the central red light before the highway reappears along
a stretch of plazas and familiar eateries. And though the tree may like a
beautiful monster seem to step out into one's path, one would be hard up
to find evidence to say that it is so and even the quick movements of one's
hands and arc around it may seem like something had suddenly stepped
out of the way. But perhaps that is how music begins to occur to us while
we imagine we aren't listening, and the dim stories brightened into focus
by inventing details until it grows into something else, and we finally have
something to say about the world, though it is opaque to us, even in the
daylight, when we look at it and finally shut up. I've been told to think
of the sun in the purity of its idea, but only feel the heat against my skin,
and see how it's made a mess of things, where the lack of light is an order
of sameness and a consistency we rely on to make judgments. Or should
we accept what they say, that the difference is the organizing principle,
though I've never been to The Apollo, only saw it on TV, what I was told
was a performance. I sat home sewn into the seams of the sofa, drinking a
Bordeaux from California, waiting for a horror movie to begin, though it
never did; it had been the day before and I seemed to survive it okay. The
tree had eaten the car and the building appeared where it wasn't supposed
to be, only to keep me waiting for a commercial I would miss anyway.
And I would never know what it was supposed to tell me about what was
happening in my way of life and how it cannot possibly help.

DIAGRAM U

A bird with purple and yellow wings

Seesawing seeing the slaughter

from the mountainside. Says

I argue with everyone I meet
and they walk over to me because I am

the floorboards and I squeak and can't shut up

Can't be shut down.

It seems that no one knows this, bird,
the air thinning as you begin to rise

The string and the ignition

Your patience, please

Dissipating, your loveless shadow
feckless meadow

Floodgate park, the bean
in the beanless pod

Sexing the now

Excrement, defilement, I have
forgotten your name

And the flame of your increment of measurement

You are the pack of cards, queen
Of clubs, queen of stabs

The downed fliers of the battle field

The cause, the rant. I have seen you
on the stage, on high grass
caustic chemicals, reactions

Of then and one and the final
peace of the tooth extraction

You are
this
falling

Flying. Into my purple
and yellow leaves

DIAGRAM V

Growing near this failure to encounter
the breathing passages opening

Never ceasing rain of experience

and dynamic lack; a drama projected
too far by exploding, by breath

isotope and its limits. Bulges of
part-blooms reasoning through

instigations called my cellar my
childhood romance, and its urges

Would the crimson you encounter
in the mirror be all your own

or does some of it belong to the sun?

Diagram W

I feel the spaceflight in these hands
and drowned long in whispering
fealty the other day

And by you glad to be resisting
reliable dog mating
traffic to fill the air

To fill the air

And arf we go

Into the blind hued matter

Motion sickness biscuits quick kiss

The river's listed

The river's listed

Exquisitely listed

Made up of knots. The panting

Diagram X

Say you have some number, some value X. It may win you a prize. It is very unlikely that it will, but that question will go unanswered while the ambiguity of the circuit remains open.

X marks the spotty and no longer virgin winter tundra, cranked oil fields of metonymy, reason's arcs and locks, all the impatient wedges added to one's portrait to avoid elective surgery. X and its many possible options, positions on the chart, career choices, when destiny lacks inevitability and the remaining contingent factors are all more or less, more or less. If your scoop of topological measurement could lift you out of the disarray, plop you back where you thought you'd belonged, you might find it an uneasy fit until the work of fitting is done and you'd be right back where you had been. It could well be that this act of fitting is destiny, or anything that might pass for it, when it is in actuality a wriggling into shape, much as we do when we are asleep, or working our way toward sleep, finding the comfort, or the appropriate discomfort to dream what we need to dream, something I will often wake up in the middle of the night amidst, unable to find the key back in. For someone in this state there is often an unfolding of the various discomforts haunting on the periphery of waking life, the ever insurgent resentments, financial woes, vague terrorisms unexplained in the body's behavior. It is your choice, go on from there—though it may not feel as though it is, the irreconcilable flows that he or she may run up against and which may just as well disappear meaninglessly for no particular reason after months of battle. It is then that we forget what we had wanted to forget all along, as if forgetting was a salve we could rely on, without calling on the x-ray, or the death ray, years of reprogramming or analysis, or whatever device might blossom on the forefront of the imagination, promising to soothe and make right, and then settle the nerves that may well be responsible for the whole absurd theater from the outset.

Of course the people of one's life weigh in significantly as well, these smooth prison officials from the workplace, for instance, with their stim-response managerial shuffle cultivated from potty training days and trumpeted into your home within as abusive hooks and jambs, walls of sound constructing a noisy fire that in the end is exceptionally unmotivating, but without which no corporate structure could possibly exist, since the very walls are made up of this fire, the heat and violence money needs to be made into more money like a rage flame accumulating in the alembic from very many sources, and because our world is driven by such agonizing, there is forgiveness all around, and as the smoke turns the rotor it dissipates and only its shadows play on screen, where we get our laughs, choking down another with dinner, at the same pitch as the central key on the keyboard. Not C, perhaps B flat, for the thing was not built symmetrically and most pieces can be played in any key, at least the basic melody, though an instrument like piano may be more difficult to transpose than say a guitar, where moving up and down the fret board easily does it. There's no worry about which white and black levers belong to the current frame. Years you can play an instrument and still not know how to play others, while some people can slip from one to another as easily as I might change my tie. She might be a young Asian woman, or a grandmother from Brussels, a bearded octogenarian with a fiddle and a hammer dulcimer. Anyone of them may have a relative recording an album in his mother's basement, playing every instrument, or sampling a few, some strings perhaps, to give the slow song the added depth a death metal band might need to sound so classic seventies. If he succeeds he makes one want to go out and hate disco all over again. Until Madonna appears, and then Prince. And it makes you wish you had continued striving toward one of your own aspirations, pick one from the bar chart, that variable of variables, like the changing weather in one's sack of flesh, one of those multitude of flavors, none of which could actually serve to transpose what it was you were feeling until it began to wonder itself to death.

What you have fealty toward one day or the next day and how it gets categorized in your bumper to bumper catalog of wants and wishes on page 17 of your organizer. But that number slips by and spreads out, becoming indistinguishable from the environment once you try to be happier with the way things have turned out so far. Like mud on the trim of your dress, the one you wore to the movies so no one could see anyway. And which one was it? Something about men on flying carpets trying to rescue children of the countryside whose parents had just been blown to bits at a wedding reception. But you love to get bombed by sipping the remaining dregs out of the glasses of the others at the party. That eventually put you in the hospital with a deadly infection, and you lost several fingertips to gangrene. Even after that you could still juggle and put back together shards of delicate pottery for exhibits at the Met and The Museum of Natural History, and you could still paint your ass off and drink deeply with the rest of the losers on 11th Street: Excene Mudraki, Angelina Farina, Dirty Lick Boy, Potty Child, Solar Baby, Jack to Die For. When you were all spindled two or three years to or fro of thirty there still seemed to be some remaining, heartwarming, youthful stupidity left in all, which you're glad you're through with, but miss quite gravely. And the election results didn't help. And that's why you decided to let the dice make decisions for you. You'd work for days filling in each of six sides with another possibility. Somehow you always got the same results. The formula stays the same and then so does the arc, that thrumming of one's own rhythm section that well-wishers cheer you on to dance to, though only through a clean break might one end up with something different, though scientifically this remains an impossibility. One has to suspect science these days; the man in the moon never once saw that coming.

Diagram Y

The mule shat in my head
eleven different diagrams

appeared to me at once

one was an old woman
carrying a basket of clay

a windshield wiper in her
briefcase made of wisteria

DIAGRAM Z

We around here aren't round, not most of us
not to the degree one might fear if he was living here.

After all it was these vibratory powers that made us so.

And from there the leaning from one side of the room
to the other in hopes of replacing one space
with a new though pre-existing
elasticity of time
so that sequences may multilayer
and drop
like soft ice cream into a cone
not any flavor
but a likeness to that span between deaths

when we sail from one idea
into another quite honestly, unconscious
of the ease of sliding (a minor preparatory note).

Whoever it was who saw us finish
should begin to unstuff the casings
from the factory jobs we are threatened with

just in case the movement isn't there to correct you.

And you are out of your house on some early July day
though when you look back on it, it is already November

and the whole chemistry of the place
has changed back
to a briefing made through a window pane.

Don't laugh. I've been here all my life
which may not have been long, but is still virtual
and for now, the hourglass is stuck

so until the next earthquake
or spending bill is signed into law
there might be something to run with that looks
more like you than you'd like to think—sorry

that it had to occur this way. More noise
is what we've invented, and that's everything
final umbrella rolled into a baton
for safe transport once dampened.

A fist of light.

And a job one can get along in.

Whoever wishes for more than that? And if they do
boy oh boy I have a feeling
they're not going to like
this movie with its moderate to inane dialog

action as terse and incomplete
as any picnic basket
without a jug of wine.

Please pass the mushrooms.

There's more than enough to go around
though several have gone off to play. And the rest?
We've already dumped their entire savings
into the kitty, laid out the cards.

After all it's a feeling thing, not something
you can wrap with the wet blanket
of the intellect, just for the sake
of having something to say. I have some Speech Soap
to wash our mouths out
just in case it turns out to be our fault
or just our shape. You don't need

any more managerial hocus now that it's
in a whip-like siege you've seen, we've all seen
before the magistrate came home, brought building
tools to add to the punishment. It's not all repetition

but it feels like it, doesn't it, the way it is
administered in an orbital motion
just before your teeth begin to loosen and the next room
sprays something painful into your eyes. Suits the ones
who've been doing it, whose music it is. They've ransacked
just about everything that's belonged to you.

And something more.

Not that you must continue to soak in it
or go off on some protracted hunt for clever vehicles
when all you really need to say is here in front of you
still attempting a reboot. If you can get no solace
from that try imagining the circle in the tesseract
or a pair of larks drawing a flaming chariot
since we have messed up our mythologies again,
construed their pageant twists of dementia to
a fairly standard narrative form, but not this.

It made sure to leave no trace to paraphrase
no bow tie for critical thinking save an endorsement
somewhat particulate in its formation over tea
a vial of lemonade for the new thinkers
and the roustabouts hanging on and wasting time.

Don't forget, it's what we're at heart engineered
to deliver, with a can of dried farts, a flame
and a quiver of darts designed to reverse the flow
of apology pearling from your lips so that it
may later be taken up, and more aggressively
as to add some grip to an eyebrow twitch.

Some may cough at such descriptions
but others will fondly remember the righteous bump
as when hurling out of car windows after a bad drunk
and one belches an epiphany swallowed
too many hours prior to relate the context
to new disciples of the ride.

Though it is only bruising in a silent and pleasing way.
That was the gist of fidelity – stormy
afternoons when who-knows-whom we'd desire
so keep a stack of records under the elm
or under the eaves for when it rains.

The drops would be plinking against a hollowed out
shingle or a leaf frizzed with filaments of heat
determined in part by the conditions
under which the genome speaks.
Though, let us not use such offensive language
among the best of us. Nay, they never liked
that explanation, too full of advanced
sophistry. But so was their spinning of the many

event horizons they've left in wakes. Each one yearns
for something once accomplished by the body, now
plastered to the past, or that which we call the past
but is no more than information written
unreliably into our senses' memory.

How fleeting life seems because these flashes are remote
intangible, though their effect on us may be operatic,
grand, even destructive in their reach,
their grasp around our present moment and bold
insistence in molding what it is our eyes see
into what the mind's eye gravitates toward. Learn to love

both the thing made and the thought that makes it, says
a quiet inner voice hanging from the chandelier
as it smokes the last
of your cigarettes, which you no longer need, since you quit
nanoseconds ago and the nicotine fit
hasn't yet wrested control of the way you decode
and transmit what you have absorbed.

It may be nothing but the results of a spoiled crust of bread
coated lightly with ergot mold. Wouldn't you be
lucky if that was all it was. Brown eyes lining
blue and green filigree around everything within reach
as those at a distance begin to quiver, since
living that way always reminded them of cleansing
and conditioning to a more finely milled set of penchants
toward nothing but the correct finger signals.

But that didn't mean they had to quit, and even though
the artifacts of the movements had grown
solitary in their organizational triumphs
a jagged tooth hooked through everything they touched

reminding of an earlier swagger,
every blemish an emblematic and caustic face
flying out of our heads
to see the sky for the first time upon the backdrop
of the moon. Wise and clever logic
all the way up the clock for braying
the impossible while still market hot
molding from ear to ear a storm,
an architecture of mad love as it's
strewn in water colors across the comics.

Someone winged and a dandy with a red cape inviting
you to feel comfortable with the level of crime
you've poured into your notebook, attempting
wholesome casuistry of roses, daffodils,
smoldering herbs and incense
and more than anything
a sound and perfunctory reason that can
parry any assault of multiple dimensions.

That's where the goddess would come in, through those
stiff cocktails of the past with their renditions
of counter heroics circling the same themes,
isotopes as if discharged from cigarette ash
to the beat of fiery lips and repeated piano knock offs
that puff up the night into phantom parallels
of your every recent fascination and fear.

It was the first face you were inclined to believe
as you sat in yesterday's demitasse night
endearing yourself to the friendly workmanship
like the coalman's daughter shoveling herself
into a straight and narrow tourniquet of a path
to have a go at the bull run while you fled

into a mountain of shattered teacups, wounding yourself
appropriately, as to avoid another spillage
before the republic was turned over to the riff raff
of the neighborhood. There you could embrace
and in that posture, hypothesize a new day.

But one needs to answer to the cyclops beneath
the staircase in that case, where he's been gathering
your resentments and heating up his spatula.
Only then will the true meaning
of this paragraph come to the fore. It's been circling
your head like a fly and grows wilder
every time you move. It knows all your afflictions
and best wishes, where meaning lacks not
the invocation of its premise, but meanders
in a beefed-up suit, not unlike the mobsters
you've met dining in midtown during the parade.

They, of course, were in several gradations,
from sparkles of light, to the thin film
over your teeth after too many days worrying.
Perhaps a hangover on the beach, eating corn chips and
frozen pizza. They don't have any more impressive
thoughts to share and to inspire you
so for the time, being what it is, you could
either collect your things and march down the runway
or continue in good faith, though the only good
reason to follow in uncertainty would be to hold
fast to faith in good faith where propriety
should perhaps lead you to some other
defunct cafeteria, for instance, in some
dead metaphysician's shop. There you can order
a dirty water dog or two, belch a few times, make fog
in the icy air left by the enlightenment.

But excuses will always suck the life out of you.
Not that anyone will tell you that at a party.
Friends will beg for you to stay, and rivals will try
to trip you out the door. It doesn't make sense
to blame anyone, since anyone could muster up
a sizable force the same as you, with one
exception: you have a right to your body and its alloys
the same as anyone; with a shield full of grommets
and holes hoisted upon it to promote
a measured permeability. Its invisible dance
to characterize, on the air, between battles, inside
a sentence with aluminum siding, a tarred roof
for viewing comets. The education system
you've been brought through smiles urbanely
with its eyes of fake fire and wry stupidity
that camps out for holiday shopping
when it is you, yourself you have failed to avoid.

This is bullshit. Standing in line is not therapy.
Neither is trying to fit my ass into this saddle.
Tote it around wherever you go and the lime
in your drink will remind you of life; you
begin to imagine running away or flying
through the wall with saw blades spinning
on your fingertips. That's how you envision
leaving your job, and on some ornate vehicle
unrecognized by the people screaming by the hole
you left. I try to shake off this tremor, but it's been
there replicating since I began these dancing lessons.
Whole tribes of us frenetically intoxicated
by a single nervous system. I've got a way
of playing cards that will undermine the government.
I have questions only I can ask because I've turned

my body into sound. It is in eighth notes and sixteenths
and triplets and various forms of collateral, from banks
bleeding through their mercy holes. I had a role in it,
a quiet, lumbering step loaded with assorted
energies. Quite the flame thrower you are, is that
kimchee you've been eating? I need to start my car.

Find out tonight whether it is really a pattern
or if seeing is the jurisdiction of some
other sensory mechanics, a passion for panic
one may presume, a handle to some other dimension
of psychic franchise ready to have you for spare change.
That's the exhumed part of the fable, anyway.
Whatever's left is as much a mystery as where
the buckshot goes. Out of the pipe like steam and into
appearance; a friendly warmth, a quiet penetration
somewhat like affection except by the mode of its chaste
benediction. I'm really in love with your data entry
the way it wiggles its way past the gate searching
for embellishments on either side of the hand
are quick movements, intoned in a circle.

We marvel at the pencil pockings, the three-pronged
equivalences, hopes barred at the opening of your
action planned was severe rental phenomenon
and now wholly possible to record. The movement backfired.
Religion is itself like that, a few scrambled heads
the rest of us starving for a music unmuddled
by insurance analysts. And as the market
betrayed itself, by trying to "know thyself" in ways
that made masturbation seem a public service
commission in comparison, mega-church after
mega-church grew out of the cesspools of all
possible worlds, to bugger us into bigger things,

an underground in wait for souls to capsize
into its one economy that sucks them off from
the podium for a few cents thrown into the basket.

You have done this before
in past lives. It is not a good idea, something
people I know will be willing to kill you about.
Forgive us yonder diner club members. We have eaten
something unsettling for young voters
trying to win by alignment to a personal
welfare state, one's name, or enter it into
that bucket of apostrophes of ownership
without the zinging final consonant attaching
one to the object of its obsession.
I have borrowed a few of the drums you've beaten
upon and they sound only hollow in my hands.
Could be the nails driven through my fingertips are not
sunk deep enough to make a difference. I am not
an actual victim, but a modeler of
victimhood, seeking out a completer sound,
though one redactive enough to insure safe use.
There are reasons why editorial pursuits like these
can begin to know themselves as progenitors
of the plausible, for an idea may be wrong
but a feeling is always might. There is a pond
we all live in. Perhaps alone. Perhaps sustained
by others. I am sorry you have to live this way.
On the surface it doesn't hurt, only beneath
the green haze of the drug, the incessant action,
bromides for the skill set, for vacillation between
the heart and the hard-headed minotaur-like marking.
No, I didn't say marketing, not yet, but I might as well
have, since any crucial difference is due, is harkened
only through the dark of framing. And once cut from

the lack of the background an *objet* loses its glitter
and its toy qualities and you no longer love it.

But behold the benevolent panther. Rocks move
out of its path as it drives down the sandy parts
of this confused tangle of secretive meditations.
Secretive because they ignore each other's
most trivial assertions. More so because
they are lying in a circle—all unframed parts
without an instruction manual lying in wait
to make useful these lying-to-each-other pieces;
and into the sky, as it suffers abdominal pain.
It begins to shift light and drop water
in hopes that you will recognize its feeling.
After all, it feels too. Who is bold enough
to enter from beneath its hips to sense its clear
aspiration, and to say it doesn't feel as you do?
Young panther, scraping across the rocks, bounding
a heresy, a fist of light, into the sky's mouth,
condom of clear wrap, of air wrap of argument
made of pieces arranged in a row. Somewhere
within that above is opinion, a choice word
grilling, a word tribe, trying to bend back the outcome,
its natural toes and the mud it has landed in.
Try not to be too simple, dark hand. You are not
letting us into your flood. We are aware of you.
Behold benevolent panther. You are an unguent
in the mouth of this trapezoidal needling,
the oblique vehicle that solidifies our love
as something more than cybernetic casserole.
Sweet darling mayhem, my chum and apprenticeship
summoning up the slag of the old spacecraft
strewn over the Mojave desert. Young predator,
benevolent killer and tearer of meat

I have choice words for you, a voice of ragtag
emblems, decals, for you, a feeling I had met
you before in another life, one of rent and drug-like
spasms, a gleeful violence. Daggered laughter
in the heart, in the syntax of your saying what
in its moment could ever have been and to find you
here, beside my bed in a tangle of shred clothing
searching for a scrap to eat, an arm, a leg
because it was you who brought us here, and you
whom we belong to, if you could loosen yourself
from my grip, from my choke hold around
what turns out to be a fuel line, a recipe book,
a collection of flavors, a memory, forgotten cause.

SECOND NATURE

MEANDERTHAL WARRIOR PRIESTESS TAKES OUT THE TRASH

A dense wall breaks under her thumbs

The pressure to relieve aches

The floor to buckle and sing alto

Dear letter writer whomever she may be

Destroyed the clock
a bit

Takes him outside as amazement vehicle

Plans to smile assertive relief already

Putting it outside with pins

Meanderthal Warrior Priestess Commutes

Signal up spine but more than average

Trouble with balance

People staring at what is held in their hands

Perhaps sleeping to the noise

And rumble of too much coffee in the machinery

Nerves fiery clutch and release nerves are

What nerves are when they begin

To choke off and offer only things to see

Not of vision; she is this metal

MEANDERTHAL WARRIOR PRIESTESS DOES A CROSSWORD

Feeling established. Like.
Reading every word.
It says. Remediation this sponge.
Library in circumference.
Believing. In Arc. It is
Transportation villain. And
So forth. Bold ties. Both
Add up to a flurry a.
Buffet of. Noxious
Lingerers. Hopefully primed
Open possible. Rem(a)inder of
Learning a lot of. Door into
Flagrant. Networks illuminated
Proximate you. Mortality. Done.

Meanderthal Warrior Priestess Changes Her Clothes

I choose to hold the hour
And not the weave, she muses
Attending to extremities
Tips of fingers and beyond
To see and not see equally
Eyes glued to unknowable
Unfathomable juice joints
Of light intersecting
What it was or becoming to be
A gash of gasses, electrons
In a lantern of guessing
What the ending fragrance should be
Calling as if a bristling sensation

Meanderthal Warrior Priestess Spends Honey on Her Self

Starting the transmission:

Back to the sting

The heartcomb

She engineers the wax
family structure
wire line of connections

From buzz to flower

Sea of air around
the moist skin
of the palm

Held out

To show what she's done

Meanderthal Warrior Priestess Shaves Her Head

Seeming whole

Broken bowl

Sets sun

Meanderthal Warrior Priestess Fixes a Flat

The pressure subsides
The wheel deformed
Requires the crisis
That she provides
Now fit for travel

MEANDERTHAL WARRIOR PRIESTESS: JOB CREATOR

Every phenomenal silence is to be filled
A breeze required to hug the body of a dead tree

Foot for shoe, step for pavement
Air to breathe and thought to think

All the crimes that fill our stories
Raised with a word from an imagined world

To build us as we are
And never otherwise be

Meanderthal Warrior Priestess Launders

Stirring conventions. The sleeping
Mist that cleans, surveys the settlement
There are no averages only peculiarities
Where she sits with her thumbs
Guiding the enterprise in its circular
Banality while claiming to instill
A valor to the fabric of validations
The interactions between you and I
She says as she watches the cycle spin

Meanderthal Warrior Priestess Justifies Her Existence

Take these parts and see if they fit

Begin with all time and narrow down to the day

It is cold and it is dark outside

Someone needs a dry hanky

A race to the center of all things in miniature

Believing it to already be vetted by a god

Or some animal under the care of a wet sun

But that is her eye holding it in place

Meanderthal Warrior Priestess Balances Her Check Book

Birds flying in and out of the windows
Help to align the air for the sound that moments
Possess as movements pass over the pen
Ink laid here and there amid the crossworks
And the dream of it all adding up. It does
Add up, all of it, but only in one of her otherworldly
Worlds, one contained in a small box she keeps
Free of ectoplasmic improvisations
Unlike the others held in softer delineations
But no matter what net she drops
There is a reaction, top to bottom
And a spice that settles on a situation
The flatness of the desk, the bulging of what appears
Upon it as the twittering releases numbers
Far more of them than was earlier imagined

MEANDERTHAL WARRIOR PRIESTESS LOUNGES

It's as difficult for some
To turn these symbols into water
As it was to begin a universe
One of similar retail value
Cradle interlocking crane
Hoisting new personalities
Into the air. It becomes dozens
Of rare minerals, exploding
Out of the ground with faces
In the direction of the stars
Asteroids colliding as she sits
In the silent radiation of suns
Saying not, hearing not, drugged
By the inevitable decay it is

MEANDERTHAL WARRIOR PRIESTESS INTERVIEWS

Very little of it is worth repeating

The natural associations are often
Unnatural. Here lies what was made

Of several hours ago while we spoke

Asserting themselves in variations: the traces

MEANDERTHAL WARRIOR PRIESTESS PUMPS GAS

This in other forms ignites a universe
Or is it belief in fiery plumes
Transcribed from nonlocal attempts
At consciousness. It nearly smells like
Something you'd want to drink
On a troubling day, one of many vectors
Converging on that intention to be real
But only a story telling other stories until an end
Of one brings an end to all
Cascadings as the digits fly on the face
Of the pump. A radio plays. The scent
Of urine mixes, weaves. A counter beat
The live and dead she straddles
With each breath, each inch of fuel
That pours into her vehicle - the flesh and steel
Strains to be awake, to continue
As a thing growing and dying. Together

THREE FICTIONS

THE NODE DANCER

Whatever have you heard the echo is rule of plastic. Down on the carpet. Up on the walls. Heaven waits for the ruffed tourniquet. There was a measure of it. All scattered. And this one a sea of shards. Of opening ups. And the other ones turning into squares. Into diagonals. A circular myth of things to come. That have already passed. Bringing the brain with them. The whole apparatus. Shimmying into a bow. A bright morning of toothbrushing and how you dos. And the books of the shelves have nothing to say. Have said all they need to say. Lumped in a corner. In a memory of having smoked, a fine morning leading to a disjunctive state. A cataclysm or a stroke of luck. And the reeling of parting and coming back together again. A thing advertised in books and movies. Like a lung breathing. Or a world and its wind. The signs of disintegration and the signs of new things coming into being. Gone are the sparrows of the intimate dialectic and come is the field of many voices uttering the same thing. With micro differences we can rely on to distinguish each voice and each mood. Each thought and its analogy to something better. Imagined better but never quite coming into place. Dissembling on one end as it assembles on the other. As fit constructions. As if energy had us playing with dark power. Since every thing destroyed as it is coming into being. Every soul, every icy stare from the other side of convenience. Convergence. For being for a brief interlude. Among the many catastrophes that inhabit life. That are the machinations of life. Because when I walk over here I have destroyed the person who stood over there. The identity that it was that was every body standing there from the beginning. Which never occurred.

Fangs and Fetishes

I went out into the world to find a healing stone. Its name was Worry. It had teeth like a snake but couldn't use them. It was a stone after all, and it didn't really have teeth. I was confusing it with a snake I wanted as a talisman. I would paint his head on the stone. Its name was Worry. I don't know why its name was Worry, but it was something to say. I went out into the desert to say it.

I went out into the desert because it was a lot different from what it is right here. I went to the desert with my feelings. I didn't know what I would find there. I went out into the desert to create the feeling of snow, though there is no snow in the desert. Not the one I'm feeling. I am the desert in my feelings and the stone is this position I must occupy. I'm on a terrace in the city overlooking the place where I belong. It is not snowing here. It is not the desert. My dog's name is not Worry.

I am the desert on my terrace here. And my dog is looking at the snow, overlooking where the snow had been because it is July in New York City. It is Brooklyn. It is different than you think. People tried explaining that to me and now I'm here. Everyone is poor in Brooklyn, no matter how much money they think they have. There are no alligators in the sewers of Brooklyn. There are trains and buses and apartments just like mine.

I am this Brooklyn I invent when I think of deserts and dream of snakes. I am this stone that heals itself, though it may look like something else. Like falling apart in bricks and stone, the dust, the wheel that blocked your way. Sitting there between two trees, a tree and snake buried in the murk, the feeling. And I crawl awake and watch the sun sugar.

DIALECTICIAN'S INSOMNIA

I left it on an ocean's wave and it never came back to me. Feels as though it never left. Forming a small patch over my kneecap serving as a second brain. A small patch traversing the entirety of my epidermis—not the physical skin, but its radiance once captured in a silver bottle now left to spread and shed itself in a soft unnoticeable glow. A warm tunic of ideas, conjectures, and or or. The metonymies work that way. They give us breadth. I left it in paradise, on the small patch cresting over a swell before it hit the shore, but it never came my way, never left me here in my disease. Became my disease and my great fortune to be here among you all tonight. As the tidal pallor thwarts us in another game of going and never receding, always in a whorl, in a knot that pursues us, gives us these alibis we call "raison d'être." As if we could ever be such a thing, except life itself walling in its warble.

The life that punishes and adheres. And it says to itself when and where but never why or what. It is out there on a wave. It is part of you never returning but always within eyes' reach, unforgettable and irredeemable. A patient island flickering on its float, and you right here with it always out of reach and by your side, imagining there is such a thing, though there is not. Something else so slippery it ceases to exist as you begin to reach.

LINES OF FLIGHT

SACRED GUARDIAN ANGEL

By the laws of perspective I grant thee

Full alliance of these linear rays, showering
In exuberance, a small flock of geese

Come to stain the window with its fluttering
Bits. The feeling of life, often punishment

Or a birthday cake, the way a kite flees
Upward, taking a small fraction of your weight

The punishment gone, transformed into
A garment of air, its beads of lumen. Some

Ruby, ochre, aquamarine, and none
By sweetened movements that pucker the breath

The square, but purely mineral eyewink
Of the engine or isotope, position of glass.

Alembic Beside the Candle

The pillar that Samson blew open with
two hairless fists—but first an adage from his
father's marketing firm, incorporated
in 1903, under the stiff wind of the Euphrates.
Before the balancing, the many killers employed
by his favorite studios, designing
chairs with a mild electric shock. The goblets
reached into the initial mayhem by sweating
mildly, engendering rings in harmony
with vibrations going through the palace
floor, on the surface of the potions the royal
family was drinking. But on the inside
of the outsideless vessel, the orchestra had
begun, sending satellite communications
in the form of asterisks and dotted lines
to all the beginning tributaries, the unlocked
hand and then its brother, slowly reaching.

Two Rocks

That one was very interesting, it said to itself, looking for the other and both exclamation marks rounded in detail.

But with every vibration they ground into each other. The sound effects are important, they said, not afraid, but contemptuous of the weather.

The sound effects are important: a small child climbing hills of fractured glass evolves into a package of operatic tensions.

Or a man who eats with his mouth made of rubber gloves strapped over headlights in dense fog, pouring rain.

The sound effects are important: the revolving light on the roof of the space-craft led us to believe so.

A tone rocked back and forth, spent and elastic on the landscape: o root magnesium of the forest.

All without function and design.

But with every vibration they ground into each other until something re-sembling a large plastic duck flew out. We were standing on the edge of the highway watching it land on the upper branches as the light on the horizon faded from red to yellow.

Neither object served a function, though they had changed as we changed. The position of our eyes.

Mouths spiraled through lists of convictions until everything was spread across the blanket, scattered among the crumbs the ants were eating. Sever-al of the children disappeared into the trees, fell out of the branches, creat-

ing a fluid dynamics. Brain synergy eats fire.
Two rocks crashing, rubbing at each other, trying to make a third thing out of two separate things.

Grinding until mouths form on both, correspondences carved, and there is a matching set, family resemblance, otherwise what would these two objects have in common besides the promiscuity of stone?

We lounge in an airport, watch yawns spread like teardrops on a sample-slide, miniature versions of the two you heard roaring in your pocket. Reliving the violence in the small, private place between your palm and fingertips. One for each eye, to excuse an other's blindness.

A matching set, and family resemblances, the shadow of the moon drawing dark grooves over a strangers face, images sunk like cities in desert fear, disappointments sharpened to carving tools, swallowed down into forgettable but disquieting compartments—

Giving off stench and smoke, wind-up music with whining cat choruses.

"Let me see them, be pretty for me."

And open wide so I too can disappear into the tide as it washes up against your sides.

Strange one from another plate or layer, we rub up and down and against each other like basalt or carbon, seeking flint, physicality of illumination.

Two rocks and red eyes falling off a swing running upstairs through a swarm of others.

The spring was said to be made of dancing things, rudimentary particles, displaced ions ripe for bonding. A clutch of animal hair reaches with pigment for rice paper or canvas, a fairy long ago in a European city, smeared and then another colliding

Distorted faces. Double vision, eyes too weak to focus on a perfect line.

I Drink this Milk

This ton of bricks moans softly as the moon
In tears begins again to envelop itself in your flood
Its ivory cup of mist, the fragrance of the bean
Pods sprouting from their vines, to spread themselves
Over your morning. And the sun dangles
From a long chain, shivers, wagging
Down among the clouds and treetops that try
To imagine themselves being so big, so warm and
Flattering, as to have a world each of their own
To pass around and trade among themselves.
The bricks sing in a chorus of muffled claps
And clusters of whispered clunks and clashes over
The way they have begun to arrange themselves
While we sip the sun and watch them dream
For us, the breeze squirreling about then screeching
And whistling, and the bricks forming sentences
Among their shadows remain nearly legible

THREE ISOMORPHS

First we have water. The attitude
Of water being one of the first principles
And imagining after that a sequence
Of translucent vehicles, all
Furbished of varying thicknesses
Of glass to travel in or over water

Lastly the air must through moistening
Become some of each, remaining
All along what it is in itself, wholly
Breathable, transporting speech
And seed pods from field to field

Milkweed, daffodil, and nectars
Lifted from flower to flower by
Bees suspended in its substance
Floating forthwith, swimming, following
Amid the eddies of its emptiness

Leap of Faith

The old lady of the sea is hiccupping ink
Her amusements are on another page
Not this one, and not the page between
As in a breath or the light flooding over
From one leaf to the next. One has to wonder
Whether she can really stop, or if it will
Depend on other factors—marbled clouds
The mechanical clasp of her belt around
The hours it's taken to be her to begin with.

She is our model and we bring her gifts
In appreciation. The gold clock, caged bird
And several fields of sheep in chains. She will
Devour them and the sun will shine and the rain
Will fall, and eventually they will be returned
To us, and we will be happy. And when
The story is over, the cry will spring again
From its cat, and that should be October.

The Felt of Right of Wrong

These button holes are dug too deep,

ex-genera as the city living in circles.
Around the pole they sweep toward

a bountiful crypt-like education
squeaking behind the headboard.

The many shirts we're taught to wear—
the quick pink ones, grey ones, orange

light dyed into fabric from evening.
The beach, in search of a miraculous

landscape divided by stars,
of doors in an arc along the entry.
Letter of your name, and what it

might mean to attempt to save you.
Save you from what? I'm the one

needs saving says the sister,
long lost beneath this head

stone where the army put it thinking
it's a long way to other general

settings, as in the piece of tape
marking the position on the dial.

I wish there was something more
intimate for us to wear. Actually

there is and I am imagining you
bringing it here in the right size.

Back in the World with You Too

If this motion sickness is the cure for therapy
and the moon won't do its tricks, how do we move mountains
when it was this twig that came out of the box,
writing its name in reverse or at least moving forward
with that thought in mind, with that reaching toward
the next moment with another set of grips.
One finds in one's suppleness a greater nervous agitation
much more successful and pleasurable,
neutralizing the ground with alkalis and arguments
that have over the centuries made us such an un-fun mob
to be around, to be spinning among our spinning and roundness
like that of the hidden circle in everything we do.
Goddess, the circle, circle majesty, as I swing my arm in an arc,
trying to kill you or touch you or invite you
into my intentions to stay. Remember who I am
and who you might be and at what point on the curve
as we speed around our bodies. Numbness and heat.
Remember the first singing I had ever done to you
and the way it revolved a heart, one we made in the middle.
We hadn't found the time and place to use tools
made of tumbling and twisting, of friction between skins,
a torrent of drumbeats pouring out of every fact.
This is how we occurred to us, and our work was complete.
Not that kind of work, but of many hammerings
breaking away the ground over which we hung, trembling
over the ground that was neither a circle nor a heart,
but a mottled flatness, an unevenness, a place to climb
or slide down into the belly or crater where it was still warm.

Flowers as Something Standing on the Counter

Waves of blue shot through my hands
and because of that I knew I had approached
a state unlike that which I was seeking,
but perhaps more useful. After all
it was a blue wave, a blue-hand waving
state I was unfamiliar with. On another day
I may have made nothing of it at all—
in fact there were days I made nothing
of it at all, and days I made still less
than that about anything that may have
happened to me—say a sudden growth spurt
or an equally fleeting decrease in size.
Because in the end it was the averaging
of these things that got me there, that place
to which I belonged, though after that it
disowned me and the flavors on my tongue
and the way I saw and thought of things.
I was in a disowned state, a flowering
and pungent yearning for that which I'd
never know, could never, not even imagine.
Standing on a lever between the window
and the open room, I ruminated long and hard,
trying to recur. Trying to be back around.

SHORT BURSTS OF CHERRY

There are roses and blood stains on these calipers.
For days I've wandered through this desert blind
and your hair was a fragrance I hadn't known yet,
blood on my hands from cutting their meat
and a soft discipline of walking with a limp.
When the sun dropping toward the horizon fell
we were beet red from heavy breathing.
The passage up the rocks was treacherous.
Thank goodness for our little friend, the doctor
who killed three guards and sucked another
of those crimson flowers, granting her vision.
Buildings of tremendous scale, some of cobble,
others of unknown origin. Grass among the ruins
and some small fruit trees and those without fruit
on the periphery—berries, small oranges and cacti crown
a flame at night but nothing more, no ghostly guide.
Flame and a sack of dried victuals still bloody from flight.
To sit and listen before faith opens her mouth,
her red O, and its first utterance, her scarlet
wordless prayer and its first reference.
The way it stabbed everyone in her bed,
everyone in her, everyone who could be counted.

Avenue X

You've taken me away from the salt breeze, taken my hand and twisted my arm—now that you're going away for the weekend what will come of my effervescence, the sting & erasure in my blood. Maybe it will be good to disappear for a while, split like a paramecium, a neuron or an atom. The memory of the poly-rhythms in your panties had been blurting out the news all night, until I misunderstood, got to flinging books around my apartment, and it was an airport with very little room to vehicle through the windows: a pencil point drifting over the mattress, leaving a line lighter than lust misconstrued. Now, if I can get my cap on I could probably remember and reassemble your name from the pieces you left me. There was an orange one, or an awning at the station, if I can remember right, and that means the police will be here some time on Sunday, or at least the holders of a policy deliberately rewritten according to a vaccination against the will. You said not to mention the names of our ordinary friends in case their makers showed up out of balance, bemused, reaching for something to salve their startled appetites. I knew it had something to do with irritation, or at least that barnacle caught on your coat after you were asleep at the beach all day.

THE CLOWN ON MY SHELF

I don't understand these feelings
Frogs jumping from one moment to the next
Releasing a kind of venom

That eases the mind. It has taken me away
To the flutter of its surgical stops
What we're committed to do

Even before the powder goes up
The red squeaky nose, and now sitting
Among the puzzles and wooden fruits

The lock box yawning its immaterial sigh.
I don't know what to do with all this vision—
I am myself wooden and small

Compared to the clutter of history
Wrestling out of the mud and now to be
Locked away without barely a trace

Only still objects, and a story
Like a profusion of moss on a skin
Because the light and its absence

Along the mottled curves, the skin
A ruptured structure of sight, or the clown
Whispering his distillate moan through each

Sensory field. Where have I remained, but
Here beside the lock box, central pushing
Without mention of its name. It was

Reasonably so; it was dense and elastic.
The wind filled with shadow and I felt good.
Little wooden man, I'd like to be a top

That spins around your head, grasping
At flight, because I don't understand these feelings
And it isn't enough just to be you anymore.

JOSEPH BEUYS IN JERUSALEM

About to rummage
Away from the mirror

Green eyes but no brow
Missing something

The science said
The telling told to it

Have no ideas
And how to arrange them

Went first to lock
The capital door

Is running out of closeness
Locks picked and this

Sentence is our savior
It said this. Thus

It said we are salving
A tantrum in a dungeon

Says like awakeness
We see the telling of

And a sup of our
How to do this part

I felt fat
Fell waxing

Onto the moon part
Olive oil and lemon

The tawny
Late afternoon sun

Still bellowing in
A felt hat

Exchanging the dark
And light like

Bodily fluids
Not body fluids

Fluids with body
Filling the sky

Yellowing nebulas
Olive and lemon oil

Bringing the that
The stars closer

So they can taste
Have scent

Washing the broken
Jaw of the heart

And magnify
Ad magnifying the

Yellow bright space
Negative of the hard

Black granules
Of crystal night

(MULTIPLES)

An object may fly apart
at hundreds of miles an hour
each particle an electric
stag of mercury whose
message is a tongue burning

(KUNST)

I remember reading
In a book on Cabala
That the true Israel
Is not a geographical location
But an omnipresence
And omnipotence
Sensate to anyone
Who would open her heart

The true Israel
Is not a hornet's nest
Between the desert
And the sea

It is capital
And true capital is art.

(Mecca)

In the Expanded
Concept of Art
True Capital is not a *what*
But a *that* you make

This the bees understand
And produce
A substance both
Form and fuel

Wax is a malleability
Like capital like vril
The self that is
Not the self alone

Or a queen who
As the ego is given
Completely to the re-
Production of the hive

Never needed are there
Two queens in one nest
Only the drone while alive
Is a multiplicity

Otherwise: a city divided
Kunst split and artificial
By a fissured jawbone
At the olive's heart

(EPICURE)

I paint with hare's blood
and lemon juice
a cannibal these days
enjoying the olives
and the almonds
I'm feeling stronger
Never do I taste the lemon
but off a pincer or pinky
the blood of Amen-Ra
Yahweh or Allah
whose secret name is Apollo
is Joseph Beuys
when in Jerusalem
at the gate of
the Kingdom of Heaven
I devolve along
with pigs and crustaceans
who with lemon
olive and a little white wine
alkeme a divine nation

Adam as a bridge
between two squirrels

The sun is out
its radius sweeping
one third of the frame

Beneath the hands
and feet of the arc
lay two elk
one living one dead

But Adam has two heads
so one cannot discern
one end from the other—
an illustration perhaps of
a single head that slides
to more than one
position—
                  one for
life and one as
its negative image
both useful
depending on intention

Much can be left
unfixed in a crude
drawing of
many lines scattered
about like grass

This is field work

(MULTIPLES)

A design for a seeding device
that blasts a hole on delivery
But does that seed take or do nearby
weeds capitalize the disruption.

Our methodologies must be tested
thoroughly when living materials
are used or the signal gets distorted
and the chaos we had hoped for

may be sacrificed for the chaos
we are trying to overcome:
a machine that repeats itself
until friction wears the bearings down

The ground collapsed
and the earth threw up

beneath us both
my body a shambles

your family deep
in snow-time

set us adrift
from quiet repose

My holy city is
a folding slate board

sprung tension between
opposing materials:

me and a coyote
in a New York City gallery

I stare at the red dot
of the sun
to see a green dot
on the head
of everyone

That way I know it's go

It's the same
with everything I do
I paint with death
(so much to spare)
to extend my breath
out past my fingertips

The honey of the world
belongs to the bees
It is their capital
and they give it freely
along with a sting
swelling red and hot
and all else is not

I stare at the red dot
of the sun
to see a green dot
on the head
of everyone

That way I know

www.ingramcontent.com/pod-product-compliance
Lightning Source LLC
Chambersburg PA
CBHW080956120626
46546CB00010B/2919